Praying with Presley

By Miss Joanne

Archway Publishing books may be ordered through booksellers or by contacting:

Archway Publishing
1663 Liberty Drive
Bloomington, IN 47403
www.archwaypublishing.com
1 (888) 242-5904

ISBN: 978-1-4808-1847-7 (sc)
ISBN: 978-1-4808-1848-4 (e)

Print information available on the last page.

Archway Publishing rev. date: 2/18/2016

A is for Ask

What am I
Supposed
To do
When I
Want to
Talk to YOU?
Should I
Bow my head
And close my
Eyes
Or
Stand up straight
And tall
And on Your name call

J
E
S
U
Says, "Be still in prayer
And I will hear all Your cares."

A is for Ask

For anyone
Who asks
Receives
And he who
Seeks finds
Matthew 7:8

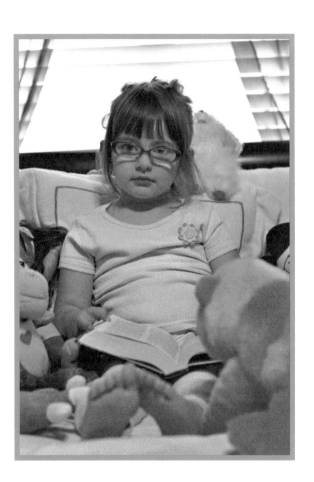

Lord Teach Me To Pray

Luke 11:1

B is for Believe
Believe in the Son

Dear Jesus, I believe You want to talk to me
I believe You care for me
I believe You hear me

"Dear Jesus, please come into my heart
because I believe in You. In Jesus name, Amen"

B is for Believe

Jesus walked on water
Jesus turned water into wine
I BELIEVE
Jesus made blind eyes to see
He made deaf ears to hear
I Believe
He made the lame to walk
He raised Lazarus from the grave

C is for Confession

If we confess our sins He will forgive our sins 1 John 1:9

Sometimes I

F
  O
    R
      G
        E
          T

my sins and

sometimes I sin

and not know it

AND

Sometimes IT'S the instant I sin

I feel   IT'S WRONG DEEP WITH IN

But

When

I confess my sins to You

I am glad You forgive   And forget them

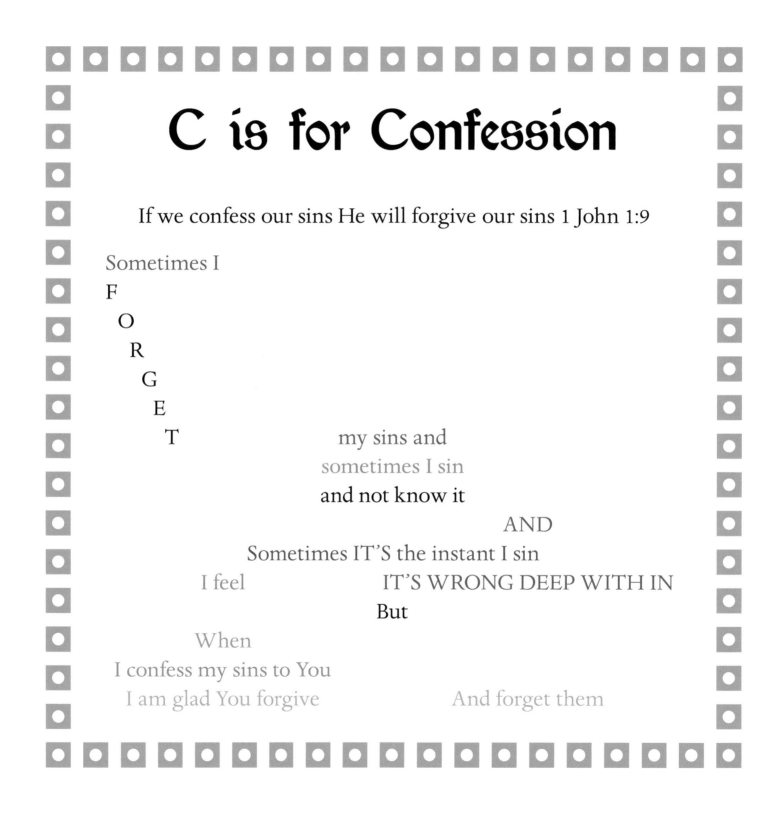

C is for Confession

GOD EXAMINE ME AND KNOW MY HEART....AND SEE
IF THERE IS ANY WICKNESS IN ME PSALMS 139:23-24

Dear God, I have learned there are consequences
when I do something bad. I am sorry, God. Amen

If we confess our sins,
He is faithful and just to forgive us our sins 1John 1:9

D is for Daily

From the rising of the sun
To its going down let the name of the Lord be praised
Praise God daily because He is
Merciful   Patient   Forgiving
All-powerful   Kind   All-knowing
Faithful and Just

The sun rises and the sun sets...Blessed
Be the name of the Lord

God, teach me to praise and worship you.

D is for Daily

"God, I love the things you have made

I will see you in the morning."

I love You

God Made

I believe God did
many miracles
but the greatest
is ME

God made the
Rainbow flowers
And the wide salty seas
So wide its end I cannot see
God made the plush green grass
And the pesky, prickly, sticking weeds
Why He made them is beyond me
God made the mommies and daddies
And the precious, cuddly babies

Who grow up to be you and me

E is for Each

Each PERSON
Each PLACE

James 5:16
When a believing person
Prays great things happen

The prayer of a righteous man is powerful and effective." Elijah was a man just like us. He prayed very hard daily that it would not rain, and it did not rain on the land for three and a half years. He prayed again for God to send rain and it did rain and the crops grew. **James 5:16-18**

E is for Each
person and place

Remember praying is you talking to God
And God listening and speaking to you.

No matter where you are gathered
At a park having a picnic or
On a mountain top or
Upon a shimmering lake
It really doesn't matter if it's
Monday Tuesday Wednesday Thursday
Friday Saturday Sunday

F is for Faith

Faith is complete belief

And when you can't see how things will work out

Presley has faith that this swing will hold her up and not let her fall. This is the same faith you need to trust in God. God will always uphold us and never let us fall.

F is for Faith
Walking and praying in faith

When Jesus went to Capernaum, a centurion came pleading to Him saying, "Lord, my servant is lying at home paralyzed. And Jesus said to him, "I will come and heal him."

The centurion answered and said, "Lord, I am not worthy that you should come under my roof. But only speak a word and my servant will be healed.

When Jesus heard this, He marveled, and said, "I say to you, I have not found such great faith not even in Israel.

Presley has faith that this swing will hold her up and not let her fall. This is the same faith we need to trust in God. God will always hold us up and never let us fall.

"Faith is complete belief and
Trust in God even when you
Can't see how things
Will work out"
I WANT TO BE
LIKE JESUS

G is for Growth

"Dear God, thank You for this day.
Thank You for Your church
So we can learn more about You."

I WANT TO BE LIKE JESUS

Jesus grew in wisdom
And in stature
And in favor with God and man

I CAN grow in wisdom
I CAN grow in stature
I CAN grow in favor
with God and man

G is for Growth

And Jesus GREW in wisdom
And in stature and in favor
with God and man.

Jesus' parents went to Jerusalem every year at the Feast of the Passover. He was twelve-years-old. When they had finished the days, the boy Jesus remained while his parents left. Joseph and Mary did not know it. When they realized Jesus was not with them, they returned to Jerusalem.

After three days Joseph and Mary found Him in the temple listening to the scholars and asking them questions. When his parents found Him, His mother said. "Son. Why have you done this to us?"

Jesus answered, "Why did you look for me? Don't you know that I must be about my Father's business?"

H is for His Word

God gave
Me His word
To teach me
He wants me
to learn

"Thank You God for our hearts
because You are inside them."

H is for His Word

If You know God's Word
You know God's Will

THY word is a
Lamp unto my
feet to guide
and to save
me from sin
and to show
me the heavenly
way. Psalm 110:11

Thy word have I hidden in my heart that I
may not sin against Thee Psalm 119:105

I is for Intersession

Intercession is a BIG word
And it is an important word
It means praying for others

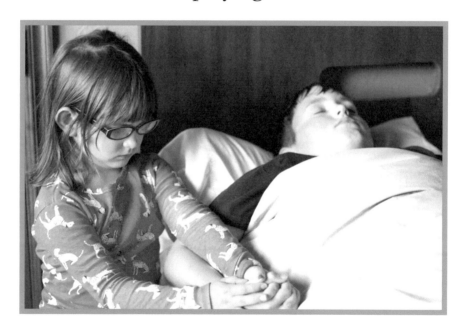

I exhort you therefore that, first of all,
supplications, prayer, intercessions and
giving of thanks be made for all men

I is for Intercession

God, for whom should I pray?

Praying for
Missionaries
Salvation
Country
Friends
Family

J is for Journey

Trust in the Lord forever
For the Lord is the Rock eternal
Isiah 26:4

My journey with God is a stream flowing over soft pebbles
and sometimes it is a roaring river rushing over large boulders

He holds
my hand along
the way
And when I rest
He gives me His
Peace and His
soft voice whispers His
love for me.

J is for Journey

As I walk down Your path, dear Lord, let my heart
be like your heart and let me trust in you always.

K is for Know

If you
Know God's Word
You Know God's will

Thy word is a lamp unto my feet
To guide and to save me from sin,
And show me the heavenly way. Psalm 119:105

Thy word have I hid in my heart that I might
not sin against thee. Psalm 119:34

Give me understanding to keep your law, to
observe it with all my heart. Psalm 119:34

"Jesus help me know what you want me to do."

K is for Know

God gave me His Word to teach me
He wants me to learn about Him
to guide me through life and
to show me His ways
I will put His words in my heart

L is for Listen

SHH I'm talking to God

Is it hard to talk to God?

No, it's
not hard
to talk to
God.
All you do
Is talk to
Him like you talk to your friends.

You say you love Him

You praise Him   You Thank Him

You listen & meditate on His Word

L is for Listen

Is it hard to talk to God?
What do I say?
How do I know He hears me?

"Dear God, I would love it to snow. I could make a snow man. God, I know you can hear me and can do everything."

Shhh God's talking to me

M is for Meditate

In His Word I meditate both day and night. Psalm 1:2

Quietly listening and
thinking about God's Word so
I can hear His small voice.

M is for Meditate

I AM BUT A CHILD
Trying to learn about prayer
When do I praise and thank God?
When do I say what I have done?

I AM BUT A CHILD
Trying to learn about prayer
When do I pray for my needs?
When do I for others plead?

I AM BUT A CHILD
Trying to learn about prayer
When is it time to meditate?
Is it that hard to keep straight?

I AM BUT A CHILD
Trying to learn about prayer
There is really no Secret

N is for Now

When should I start to pray?

N is for Now

If I am 5
Can I begin to pray or
Maybe I have to wait
for
8
I'm really not certain of the age
Or place but
I'm going to start Now
Isn't that great

May I never get so busy for You that I
neglect time with You. Luke 10:38-40

O is for Opportunity

pray to watch for opportunities

privately in your own little closet

one prayer at a time

room in your heart for accepting His timing

time everyday

us to grow in Godly character

needs will be met

in grace, knowledge, understanding

truly grow in God's character

you after His heart

O is for Opportunity

"Dear God, I had such a busy day.
And now it's time to say, "Goodnight"
But wait! I didn't take time to talk to you
I meant to, but I let things get in my way
I cleaned my room and played with my dolls
Tomorrow will be better."

GOD, AS I LIE DOWN AND GET READY
FOR SLEEP, THANK YOU FOR WATCHING OVER ME.
THANK YOU FOR THE STARS THAT
ARE SHINING UP ABOVE. GOOD NIGHT

P is for Praise

For great is the Lord and most worthy of praise

When I sing, I hear the melody
I wonder what God hears?
When I read the Bible, I hear
my voice
I wonder what God hears?
When I pray, I hear my words
I wonder what God hears?

P is for Praise

GOODNESS

HOLINESS

MERCY

JUSTICE

When I Praise God
He Sings Along

Q is for Quiet Time

Be still and listen
We need to talk To God
Everyday
Grammy says,
It's called, "a quiet time"
And to pray
For others and for myself
A time to hear God's still small voice
And where do I go to close out the noise
My bedroom has a big closet
I could sit in there
And talk all I want for no one can hear
BUT GOD

Q is for Quiet Time

When we pray we talk to God
When we are still God talks to us.

When you pray, go into your room and when
you have shut your door, pray to your Father
who is in the secret place. . .Matthew 6:6

R is for Ready

Who Am I
That God is mindful of me
When God is so **BIG**
AND I am so small
I can call on Him
When no one is stirring
I can call on Him
In the clearest of mornings
I can call on Him in darkest of nights
Who am I that God is mindful of me

Thou wilt keep me in perfect peace
when my eyes are upon You.
Stand in awe, and sin not: commune with your own
heart upon your bed, and be still. Selah. Psalm 4:4

R is for Ready

God is always ready for me to talk to Him
So I go to Him again
And again

Who am I that God is mindful of me?

Talk to God any time, any place, anywhere

What is man that You are mindful of him? Hebrews 2:6

Dear Lord, I love You in the morning because
you keep me safe through the night

S is for Start

God is always ready for me to talk to Him
So I go to HIM again and again
Who am I that God is mindful of me

Talk to God any time, any place, anywhere
What is man that You are mindful of him Hebrews 2:6

Dear Lord, I love You in the morning because
You keep me safe during the night

S is for Start

to

pray

today

God is waiting for you

"Dear God, my creator of everything
and the Cubbies' motto
" Jesus loves me,"
reminds me that I love my family and friends."

T is for Thanksgiving
1 Corinthians 13:4

"Dear Jesus, I pray that I always say nice words. I love you because you love us. Amen. I'm going to eat my breakfast now then snuggle with my Mom because I'm cold and still tired. I love You, God, and thank You for my cereal you made. Amen."

Praying to Jesus is like eating a banana split.
The whipped cream is the best.
Just like You, Jesus
Then don't forget the three scoops--
separate scoops but all in one.
The foundation 0f the split
And Oh, don't forget the three flavors
Chocolate   strawberry   marshmallow
Like the Trinity separate flavors but one job
And the best part
Is getting ready to start

T is for Thanksgiving

"Thank You God For my Gram
Jesus and God
Thank You For my Moma and
Daddy and,

PAWPA"

Give thanks to the LORD, for He is good; His love endures forever.
1 Chronicles 16:3

Oh, give thanks to the Lord, for He is good! For His mercy endures forever. **Psalm 107:1**

U is for Understand

Let us come before his presence with thanksgiving.
Let us shout joyfully to Him with Psalms for
the LORD is a great God. Psalm 95:23

No matter how young I am
You will help me understand
How to pray
I don't have to always
Bow my head
And utter certain words to say
You have made Me free to come to you
When I'm in bed
Or if I'm walking on a busy street
You promised You will be with me always
And never never leave me or forsake me
That makes me very very glad
That I have a friend like You

U is for Understand

God, do you really understand me when I disobey my parents?

Thou shall honor your father and mother

When I tell a lie?

Thou shall not lie

When I don't like SOMEONE?

Love thy neighbor as yourself

God, I don't understand your ways, but I will obey.

V is for Voice

Have you ever heard God's voice?
I wonder what it's like
Is it quiet as the purr of a kitten
Or **loud** like the roar of the lion
Does He speak to you in your dreams like
Joseph and you brag to your brothers
Or does He call you like Samuel
"Samuel, Samuel"
And will you reply,
"Here am I' or
Will you hear him in a burning bush
like Moses and You reply
"Who am I"
No,
His still small voice is heard
today when you're in prayer
and when you're in His Word

V is for Voice

He will speak to me.
Do you Remember
The story about Elijah

Elijah thought he was all alone in believing in God. Then God said, "Go out, and stand on the mountain before the Lord."

And behold, the Lord passed by, and a great and strong wind tore into the mountains and broke the rocks in pieces before the Lord, but the Lord was not in the wind, and after the wind an earthquake, but the Lord was not in the earthquake and after the earthquake a fire, but the Lord was not in the fire, and after the fire a still small voice.

W is for Worship

Our Father who is in
Heaven
Holy is Your name
Luke 11:2

"Thank You for my family and friends
Because You save everyone"

1 Thessalonians 5:18

W is for Worship

You are w**O**nderful

whispers in **T**he night

Y of praise

W**O**R**T**H**Y** w

praise

s

e

X is for eXtra Time

Even a child is known by His doing Prov. 22:11

T
I
M

X is for eXtra Time

"Father God, teach me
To give you thanks
and praise at all times."
1 Thessalonians 5:18

Y Is for Yield
To Give Up Something or Someone

Dear God,
As I play with my
friends
Let me be nice
and not mean.
Help me to act
in a way
that is pleasing
to you

God is always
GLORIFIED
When we yield
To HIM

Z is for Zeal

Romans 12:11-12

Never be lacking in zeal….

Be faithful in prayer

Z is for Zeal
For God's Word

A Child's Prayer

I am but a child
Trying to learn about prayer

I know of no right or wrong way
To talk to God

I just have to speak to Him
As I would speak to Gram

And then listen for Him to speak
To me in His small soft voice

An Encouraging Word to Parents

Parents, it is important for you to help guide your children in learning and putting into practice the principles of prayer. In a day when so many families are under attack, God's word provides a pattern for protection and victory. That pattern is centering families around God and His word. Current conditions have become so severe, parents must take this subject seriously or lose their children to the world's evil designs. According to the Bible, parents must take the primary responsibility to pray for, protect and guide their children. While the church is vitally important, it cannot replace consistent prayer and teaching at home. In the face of modern pressures, many parents feel intimidated by the subject of teaching their children to pray.

This tool is designed to help you guide your children to learn about prayer. It is a simple and flexible tool designed to teach about prayer.

Printed in the United States
By Bookmasters